THE FRAGRANCE

When Obedience Becomes Worship

Oluwakemi T. Amuda

COPYRIGHT PAGE

The Fragrance: When Obedience Becomes Worship

Published by **Kemi A. Global Press**

Manhattan, New York

Scripture quotations are from the Holy Bible and are used respectfully for teaching and spiritual edification.

ISBN: 979-8-9956458-4-9

Cover Design: Kemi A. Global Press

Printed in the United States of America

DEDICATION

To God the Father, Jesus the Son, and
to the Holy Spirit, who turned that yes into
oil,
and that oil into fragrance.

And to every surrendered vessel that obeys
God,
even when no one is watching.
This book is for you.

ACKNOWLEDGMENTS

To every person who has walked with me, prayed for me, challenged me, or believed in me, thank you. Your presence has been a quiet strength, a steady light, and a reminder that obedience is never walked alone.

To the women who carry oil, to the men who carry fire, to the leaders who carry vision, and to the silent worshippers whose obedience fills rooms without applause, you are the hidden pillars of this generation.

To my family, whose love is a covering and whose faith is a legacy, your lives are a fragrance that shaped mine. And to the Holy Spirit, the Breath behind every word, the Whisper behind every revelation, the Presence that turns ink into life, thank You.

PREFACE

There are moments when God speaks, and the world around you remains motionless. No wind shifts; no sound traverses the air. Nonetheless, an internal awareness persists that a Voice has traversed your spirit. It is an audible silence, a silence that captivates, stabilizes, and imparts a profound understanding that defies explanation. This publication was conceived in that silence, not from noise.

Not from striving.

Not from ambition.

Nevertheless, stemming from an unwavering whisper that persisted, it is apparent that throughout Scripture, divine communication was conveyed through diverse methods, including burning bushes, angels, dreams, prophets, storms, and animals. However, the medium was never the primary concern; instead, it was the Voice itself. Each time God articulated, transformations occurred: hearts were awakened, lives were redirected, and destinies were unlocked.

Yet, one verity exceeds all others: obedience constitutes the essence of reverence. Abraham apprehended this atop the mountain. The woman bearing the alabaster box recognized it at Jesus' feet. Jesus Himself demonstrated this in Gethsemane.

This book is not a theological

dissertation. It is not a religious manual. It is a spiritual revelation. It is intended for those who have heard God's whisper and pondered their next course of action. It is for those who perceive that worship extends beyond songs and ceremonies.

It is for those who yearn to obey but struggle with surrender. It is for those who desire to know God, not from afar, but in truth. May these pages awaken your discernment, soften your heart, and draw you into the kind of obedience that becomes worship and the kind of worship that becomes a fragrance rising to God.

EPIGRAPH

"Every act of obedience releases a fragrance only heaven can measure." - Kemi

AUTHOR'S NOTE

This is not a book of theory.

It is a book of encounter.

So, read slowly.

Read prayerfully.

Read with expectation.

Each chapter arrived as a whisper, a stirring, a weight, and a fragrance that persistently lingered until it was articulated. Obedience is not glamorous; it is not ostentatious, and it is not always comprehended.

However, it is sacred, serving as the foundation where worship metamorphoses into life.

At the end of each chapter, you will find a prayer,

not to close the chapter,
but to open your spirit.

Let the Holy Spirit breathe on every word.
Let Him speak between the lines.
Let Him awaken the fragrance within you.

If these pages touch you, it is not because of my words;
it is because the Holy Spirit breathed through them.

May this book follow you.
May it interrupt you.
May it call you.

May it comfort you.
May it commission you.
And may it leave a fragrance on your life that cannot be washed away.

Oluwakemi T. Amuda

INTRODUCTION

Worship has been misunderstood.

We have surrounded it with melodies, dimmed lighting, raised hands, and emotionally charged moments. We have established stages for its expression, developed language around it, and rendered it into a performance. However, long before the existence of instruments, choirs, or worship teams, worship was solely characterized by one concept: obedience.

When Abraham told his son, “We are going to worship,” he wasn’t carrying a song. He was carrying a knife. When the woman broke her alabaster box, she didn’t sing a hymn. She shattered her pride. When Jesus prayed in Gethsemane, He didn’t lift His hands in a chorus. He yielded His will.

Worship is not sound. Worship is surrender.

Worship is yielding.

Worship is obedience. And obedience always releases a fragrance.

This book explores the fragrance of the invisible aroma that emanates from a life harmonized with God. It is characterized by the scent of trust, surrender, and the recognition and embrace of one's identity and calling. This fragrance endures well beyond the act of obedience. Each chapter is initiated with a question, as worship invariably commences with such inquiry: Will you obey? Will you trust? Will you yield?

And each chapter ends with a question,

because worship always leaves you with something to ponder, something that follows you into your day, your decisions, your relationships, your destiny.

This is not a long book.

It is a precise one.

A prophetic one.

A fragrance in written form. And if you let it, it will awaken something deep within you, something ancient, something holy, something that has been waiting for your yes.

Table of Contents

PART I

THE CALL TO SURRENDER

CHAPTER ONE

THE AUDIBLE SILENCE: WHEN GOD SPEAKS

There is a silence that is not void. It is not characterized by the lack of sound, but rather by the presence of a Voice that refuses to compete with noise. It is the kind of silence that enters a room before you realise it, settles on the heart before it can be identified, and captivates the mind without necessitating acknowledgement. Such silence is not passive; it is deliberate. It embodies the language of God when He elects to communicate without words.

How does one discern the voice of God when He does not speak audibly? How does one recognize Him when there is no thunder, no angelic visitation, no dream, no vision, only a stirring, a pull, a knowing? Scripture calls this “a still small voice” (1 Kings 19:12), a whisper that carries weight, a breath that carries instruction, a silence that carries Presence. It is the voice that does not shout yet cannot be ignored, the voice that does not force yet cannot be mistaken by the heart that is willing to listen.

Throughout Scripture, God has spoken in ways that transcend human expectations. He communicated with Moses through a bush that was aflame yet not consumed. He summoned Samuel during the night with a familiar voice. He approached Elijah not through the wind, earthquake, or fire, but in a whisper following the storm. He addressed

Mary with an angelic greeting and guided Joseph through visions in dreams. He confronted Paul with a blinding light that illuminated his understanding. Different vessels, different methods, yet the same Voice, consistent, unwavering, unmistakable.

Whenever God speaks, a transformation occurs. A heart is awakened, a destiny is altered, and a life is redirected. An aroma begins to ascend. Jesus stated, "My sheep hear My voice, and I know them" (John 10:27). His voice may not always be loud; however, it is always perceptible to the heart that has learned to remain still. Discernment functions as the ear of the spirit, representing the capacity to recognize God in the ordinary, the unexpected, the quiet, and the subtle. It is the grace to affirm, "This is Him." Stillness enables the soul to perceive what the natural ear cannot, as it is written, "Be still, and know that I am God" (Psalm 46:10).

People often assume God is silent because they expect Him to act like a man, yet Scripture says, "God is not a man" (Numbers 23:19). His ways are not our ways, and His thoughts are not our thoughts (Isaiah 55:8–9). He speaks in stillness, as He did with Elijah, "a still small voice" (1 Kings 19:12). He speaks in thunder, "The God of glory thunders" (Psalm 29:3). He comes with fire, "For the Lord your God is a consuming fire" (Deuteronomy 4:24). He speaks through creation, "Day unto day utters speech, and night unto night reveals knowledge. There is no speech nor language where their voice is not heard" (Psalm 19:1–3). He speaks again and again, but "man perceives it not" (Job 33:14). God has never been silent; we are simply distracted. We miss His voice because we expect Him to sound like us, when Jesus already said, "My sheep hear My voice" (John 10:27).

Abraham understood this silence. When God said, "Take your son," Abraham heard more than an instruction. He heard an invitation. He heard worship. He heard destiny unfolding inside a single command. God never said, "Worship Me," yet Abraham discerned that obedience is worship. This is the mystery of the audible silence: God's voice does not always explain; it often invites. It often tests. It often reveals what is within us. And when we obey, something rises from our lives, something invisible, something holy, something God receives as worship. A fragrance. The fragrance of trust. The fragrance of surrender. The fragrance of obedience.

This is where worship begins, not in music, not in emotion, not in atmosphere, but in the moment you say yes to the voice you cannot ignore. Worship is not the song you sing; it is the life you yield. It is the obedience you offer when no one is watching. It is the sacrifice you make when no one applauds. It is the truth you stand in when no one understands. Worship is spirit and truth, and truth is costly. Truth demands obedience. Obedience demands sacrifice. And sacrifice releases fragrance. So the question is not whether God is speaking. The question is whether we have stilled ourselves long enough to hear Him. What has God whispered to you in the silence that you have not yet obeyed?

What fragrance has yet to rise from your life because obedience has been delayed?

Prayer:

Lord, teach me to hear You in the quiet. Still my soul until Your whisper becomes my anchor, my compass, and my peace. Let every lesser voice fade until only Yours remains.

CHAPTER TWO

THE WOMAN NO ONE SAW: IDENTITY HIDDEN BY SHAME

What happens when God sees what everyone else has overlooked, including the person themselves?

There are instances in Scripture in which God's gaze becomes the pivotal moment in an individual's life. Not His voice. Not His miracle. His gaze. The manner in which He observes a person who has remained unnoticed for an extended period. The way He perceives identity beneath layers of history, failure, and shame. Scripture states, "Man looks at the outward appearance, but the Lord looks at the heart" (1 Samuel 16:7). When God observes, He perceives what others are unable to see. He perceives what shame has endeavoured to conceal. He perceives what destiny has been waiting to unveil.

The woman with the alabaster jar entered at such a moment. She moved into the room quietly, almost apologetically. Not due to a lack of presence, but because shame had been her instructor for years. Shame teaches an individual to diminish oneself. It teaches them to enter a space without causing disturbance. It instructs them to believe that their past is more prominent than their purpose. People observed her reputation. People observed her mistakes. People observed the labels associated with her story. However, no one observed her.

Except Jesus.

The Scripture introduces her simply: "A woman came with an alabaster jar of very expensive perfume" (Mark 14:3). No name. No title. No description. She is characterized solely by her possession, not by her identity. This exemplifies the effect of shame. It diminishes personal identity to mere objects. It conceals purpose within history.

It persuades an individual that they are the aggregate of their failures. However, God perceives beyond human limitations. Jesus looked beyond the jar, beyond the whispers, beyond the reputation, and beyond the wounds.

He perceived the fragrance prepared to be unveiled. She entered the room, trembling, but she entered. That was her first act of obedience. Before the jar broke, her will broke open. Before the perfume filled the room, her courage filled her steps. Sometimes obedience begins with simply showing up in a place shame told you to avoid. Sometimes worship begins with the decision to walk towards Jesus when everything in you wants to hide.

She positioned herself behind Him, and a sense of reverence commenced to elevate within her. Her sense of identity was awakened, not the identity conferred by others, nor the one she sought to conceal, nor the one her past endeavoured to define. It was the identity that God has invariably known. When she broke the jar, she was not merely expressing perfume; she was relinquishing herself, her surrender, her acts of worship, her bravery, and her authentic name. The Scripture states, “She broke the jar and poured the perfume on His head” (Mark 14:3). The act of breaking the jar was an integral part of her worship. Pouring was an integral part of her surrender.

The fragrance served as evidence of her obedience, and Jesus received it. He did not recoil. He did not judge. He did not remind her of her past. He did not allow others to diminish her offering. He defended her. “Leave her alone,” He said. “Why are you bothering her? She has done a beautiful thing to Me” (Mark 14:6). Beautiful. Not sinful. Not shameful. Not inappropriate.

Beautiful. With one sentence, Jesus restored what shame had stolen. Her act of surrender became her introduction.

Her obedience became her identity. Her fragrance became her legacy.

And the woman no one saw became the woman Jesus said would be remembered "wherever the gospel is preached throughout the world" (Mark 14:9). Shame hid her. Obedience revealed her. Worship renamed her. Fragrance immortalised her.

The question is no longer, "Who was she?"

The question is, **"What part of you has shame tried to hide that God is now calling into the light through obedience?"**

Prayer:

Father, give me the courage to obey You even when it costs me. Break fear, break hesitation, break pride. Let my yes rise before You like incense, pure, surrendered, unwavering.

CHAPTER THREE

THE ALABASTER BOX: WHAT WE PROTECT INSTEAD OF SURRENDER

What are you holding so tightly that God cannot use it until you break it?

Every individual possesses an alabaster box. It may not be sculpted from stone or filled with fragrance. It may not be displayed on a shelf or visible to others. However, it exists quietly and privately and is fiercely defended. It is the aspect of oneself that is protected, the part of the individual that is unwilling to be revealed, the fear that is concealed, the identity that is held tightly, and the narrative believed to define them. It is the one element held firmly, even when divine authority demands it.

For the woman in Scripture, the alabaster box was her most valuable possession. It held the remnants of her past, the fragments of her identity, the security she clung to, the reputation she carried, and the story she had lived. It was the one thing she could still control in a life that had often slipped beyond her control. Scripture states, "A woman came with an alabaster jar of very expensive perfume" (Mark 14:3). This jar represented everything she had been, everything she feared, everything she protected.

Human beings are no different. Some defend pride because it shields them from vulnerability. Some people fear safeguards because they feel safer than hope. Some preserve a relationship, a dream, a talent, a wound, a secret, a plan, or a version of themselves they refuse to relinquish alabaster box becomes whatever a person guards instead of surrenders. It becomes the object they hold close, even when God is asking for it.

But Scripture does not say she opened the jar. It says, “She broke the jar and poured it on His head” (Mark 14:3). She did not unscrew it gently. She did not measure the offering. She did not drizzle it carefully. She broke it. Because some things cannot be surrendered gradually. Some things cannot be released politely. Some things cannot be offered in pieces. Some things must be shattered.

Breaking is violent. Breaking is final. Breaking is irreversible. Breaking is obedience in its purest form. And breaking is worship. The jar had to break for the fragrance to escape. The act of surrender had to be complete for the offering to rise. The woman's obedience had to cost her something for it to carry weight. This is why surrender feels painful, because something must be broken for something greater to be released.

When she broke the jar, she was not merely releasing perfume. She was releasing herself. Her pride cracked open. Her fear dissolved. Her shame lost its grip. Her reputation fell away. Her self-protection shattered. And in that breaking, she found freedom. The fragrance filled the room, not because she possessed perfume, but because she possessed courage. The fragrance was not in the jar. The fragrance was in the breaking.

This is the deep truth: what a person refuses to break becomes their prison. What they break before God becomes their worship. The alabaster box was never created to remain whole. It was designed to be broken. So are the things we cling to. God does not ask for the jar. He asks for the breaking. He asks for the moment when surrender becomes more important than control, when obedience becomes more valuable than safety, when worship becomes more costly than pride.

Your obedience is the key. Your surrender is the release. Your breaking is the fragrance that rises before God.

What is God asking you to break so that the fragrance of your life can finally be released?

Prayer:

Break open what I've been protecting. Pour out what I've been withholding. Let nothing in me remain sealed when You are worthy of all. Make my life a fragrance poured at Your feet.

PART II

THE JOURNEY OF OBEDIENCE

CHAPTER FOUR

ABRAHAM'S MOUNTAIN: WHEN OBEDIENCE BECOMES WORSHIP

What if the greatest act of worship in your life is the one that costs you the most?

What if the greatest act of worship in your life is the one that costs you the most? When Abraham climbed the mountain, he did not go there to sing. He did not go to pray, to perform a ritual, or to create a moment. He went for one reason alone: he went to obey. God had spoken, and the instruction was painfully clear. "And he said, Take now thy son, thine only son Isaac, whom thou lovest, and get thee into the land of Moriah; and offer him there for a burnt offering upon one of the mountains which I will tell thee of." (Genesis

22:2). There was no explanation, no comfort, no details, no promise of what would happen next. Heaven gave him direction, not reassurance.

Yet Abraham discerned something deeper. He recognized the Voice that had called him out of Ur. He recognised the weight that always accompanied divine instruction. He recognized the invitation hidden inside the command. So, when he turned to his men and Isaac and said, “And Abraham said unto his young men, Abide ye here with the ass; and the lad and I will go yonder and worship, and come again to you.” (Genesis 22:5), he revealed a truth that still shakes the world: obedience is worship.

Not the song. Not the atmosphere. Not

the emotion. Not the moment. Obedience.

Abraham carried wood, not a melody. He carried fire, not a psalm. He carried a knife, not a chorus. And yet heaven called it worship. Because worship is not what a person does with their hands; it is what they do with their heart. Worship is not the sound they make; it is the surrender they give. Worship is not performance; it is posture.

On that mountain, Abraham's obedience revealed his true character. It demonstrated his trust in God, his identity as a bearer of the covenant, his calling as the father of nations, his surrender to divine will, his courage to venture into the unknown, and the aroma of his faith ascending before God.

Indeed, aroma, because obedience

consistently releases an influence into the atmosphere of an individual's life. It transforms the environment. It modifies the spiritual climate. It proclaims to both heaven and hell that God is of greater worth than the object being surrendered. Isaac asked, “Where is the lamb for the burnt offering?” and Abraham answered, “God Himself will provide the lamb” (Genesis 22:7–8). That was not certain. That was surrender. That was the fragrance of trust rising before the provision appeared.

As Abraham lifted the knife, heaven responded. “And he said, Lay not thine hand upon the lad, neither do thou any thing unto him: for now I know that thou fearest God, seeing thou hast not withheld thy son, thine only son from me." (Genesis 22:12). Not due to God's unawareness, but because obedience unveils truths that words cannot articulate. Obedience demonstrates what belief merely asserts. It affirms what the heart genuinely possesses. In that moment of surrender, God revealed the elevation: "Then Abraham lifted his eyes and looked, and there behind him was a ram caught in a thicket" (Genesis 22:13). Provision resides in the realm of obedience. A promise is reaffirmed. A destiny is sealed. A legacy is established.

Abraham obeyed, and God provided.

This is the pattern woven through Scripture. This is the pattern of worship. This is the pattern of every life that chooses surrender. Obedience unlocks provision.

Obedience reveals identity. Obedience activates calling. Obedience breaks limitations. Obedience becomes worship. And worship becomes fragrance. The mountain was never about Isaac. It was about Abraham. It was about what obedience would reveal in him. It was about the fragrance that would rise from his surrender. It was about the kind of worship that costs something, because only costly worship carries weight.

Your mountain is the same. God is not trying to take something from you; He is trying to reveal something in you. He is calling you into a place where obedience becomes the fragrance of your worship, where surrender becomes the altar, and where trust becomes the offering.

What is God asking you to place on the altar so that obedience can become the fragrance of your worship?

Prayer:

Lord, lead me up the mountain of obedience. Teach me to trust You when I cannot see the ram in the thicket. Let my worship be proven not by words, but by surrender.

CHAPTER FIVE

THE BREAKING: YIELDING AS THE PATH TO SURRENDER

Why does surrender feel impossible until your heart finally yields?

Surrender is never the first step. It is always the second. Before anything breaks on the outside, something must soften within. Before the alabaster jar shattered in the woman's hands, her heart had already yielded. Before Abraham lifted the knife on the mountain, his spirit had already bowed. Before Jesus whispered, "Not My will, but Yours be done" (Luke 22:42), His humanity had already bent under the weight of the Father's plan.

Yielding is the quiet moment before the breaking. It is the internal yes before the external act. It is the place where obedience becomes possible. Many people try to surrender without yielding, and that is why they struggle. Surrender without yielding becomes performance, an action without alignment.

Yielding without surrender becomes intention, desire without completion. But yielding that leads to surrender becomes worship. Yielding is the softening of the heart, the moment when resistance melts, when fear loosens its grip, when pride bows, when the will bends toward God.

It is not dramatic.

It is not loud.

It is not visible.

It is internal, invisible, sacred.

It is the moment God sees before anyone else sees anything.

This is why Scripture warns, “Harden not your hearts” (Hebrews 3:8). A hardened heart cannot yield. And a heart that cannot yield cannot surrender. And a life that cannot surrender cannot worship. This is why obedience feels heavy until the heart yields. This is why surrender feels painful until the spirit softens. This is why breaking feels impossible until the will bends.

The woman with the alabaster jar did not break it out of impulse. She broke it because her heart had yielded to God’s pull long before her hands touched the jar.

Scripture says, "She broke the jar and poured the perfume on His head" (Mark 14:3). The breaking was not the beginning of her worship; it was the evidence of it. Her heart had bowed before her body moved.

Abraham did not climb the mountain out of duty. He climbed it because his heart had yielded to the voice of God before his feet took a single step. When God said, "Take now your son…" (Genesis 22:2), the breaking began inside him. The mountain was only the outward expression of an inward surrender.

Jesus did not surrender His will in Gethsemane out of obligation. He surrendered because His heart had yielded to the Father's purpose before the cross ever touched His shoulders. His yielding made His obedience possible. His obedience made His sacrifice complete. His sacrifice released the fragrance of redemption into the world.

Yielding is the birthplace of obedience. Yielding is the womb of surrender. Yielding is the soil where worship grows. And when the heart yields, breaking becomes easy. Not painless, but easy. Because the hardest part is never the breaking. The hardest part is the yielding.

Once the heart yields, the jar breaks naturally.
Once the heart yields, the knife lifts willingly.
Once the heart yields, the will bows freely.

Yielding is the quiet miracle that makes surrender possible.

Where is God asking you to yield so that surrender can finally become possible?

Prayer:

Holy Spirit, release the aroma of Christ through my life. Let every place of yielding become a place of encounter. Make my surrender a testimony that draws others to You.

CHAPTER SIX

THE FRAGRANCE: WHAT OBEDIENCE RELEASES

What rises from your life when you obey God in ways no one else sees?

Fragrance is invisible, yet undeniable. You cannot touch it, but you can feel it. You cannot hold it, but it fills the room. You cannot see it, but it changes the atmosphere. This is what obedience does. When the woman broke her alabaster jar, Scripture says, "The house was filled with the fragrance of the perfume" (John 12:3). The fragrance did not remain in the jar. It did not cling only to her hands. It did not stay contained at the feet of Jesus. It filled the room.

Obedience always fills the room. Not the physical room, the room of a person's life.

The room of their destiny.

The room of their relationships.

The room of their calling.

The room of their future.

Obedience unleashes an intangible essence that transcends human fabrication, an essence acknowledged by the heavens and impossible for the world to disregard. The fragrance symbolises the manifestation of surrender, the testament to yielding, and the aroma of trust ascending before God. Scripture describes this as "a sweet-smelling aroma, an acceptable sacrifice, well pleasing to God" (Philippians 4:18).

Abraham released a fragrance on the mountain when he lifted the knife in obedience. God said, "Now I know that you fear God" (Genesis 22:12). Jesus released a fragrance in Gethsemane when He surrendered His will to the Father, praying, "Not My will, but Yours be done" (Luke 22:42). The disciples released a fragrance when they left everything to follow Him. Paul released a fragrance when he declared, "I count all things as loss for the excellence of the knowledge of Christ" (Philippians 3:8).

Every act of obedience carries a scent.

A scent of faith, a scent of courage, a scent of sacrifice, a scent of devotion, a scent of worship. And here is the mystery: the fragrance outlives the act. The woman's act lasted a moment, but her fragrance has lasted generations. Abraham's obedience lasted a day, but his fragrance has lasted millennia. Jesus' surrender lasted a night, but His fragrance has filled eternity.

This is why obedience matters.

This is why surrender matters.

This is why yielding matters. Because what a person does in a moment becomes a fragrance that lingers long after they are gone. Your obedience today becomes someone's breakthrough tomorrow. Your surrender today becomes someone's healing tomorrow. Your yielding today becomes someone's revelation tomorrow.

Fragrance becomes legacy.

Fragrance becomes impact.

Fragrance becomes worship, rising beyond the moment.

And here is the deepest truth of all: the fragrance is not the perfume. The fragrance is the obedience. The jar was only the vessel. The perfume was only the symbol. The fragrance was the worship.

Your life is the jar.
Your obedience is the perfume.
Your worship is the fragrance rising before God.

What fragrance is rising from your obedience right now, and who might it be reaching beyond your sight?

Prayer:

Break me only in the places that lead to healing. Shatter what keeps me from You. And from the fragments, let Your glory rise.

PART III

THE TRANSFORMATION OF WORSHIP

CHAPTER SEVEN

WORSHIP AS SURRENDER: BEYOND SONGS AND PERFORMANCE

Have we mistaken the sound of worship for the substance of worship?

Worship has become routine, predictable, and commodified. We are aware of the chords that evoke emotion, the language that appears sacred, and the atmosphere that indicates reverence. We understand how to orchestrate a moment. However, moments do not constitute worship. Music itself is not equivalent to worship. Emotion alone does not define worship.

Worship is surrender.

Long before the advent of musical instruments, the formation of choirs, or the establishment of stages in churches, worship was fundamentally a posture rather than a performance. Abraham engaged in worship with a knife in his hand as he ascended a mountain in obedience.

Jesus engaged in worship with a surrendered will as He bowed in Gethsemane, praying, "Not My will, but Yours be done" (Luke 22:42).

None of them sang.
None of them lifted their hands.
None of them had an audience.

Their worship was obedience.
Their worship was surrender.
Their worship was costly.

True worship always costs something. It costs pride. It costs control. It costs comfort. It costs certainty. It costs the version of ourselves we have been protecting. This is why Jesus said, “But the hour cometh, and now is, when the true worshippers shall worship the Father in spirit and in truth: for the Father seeketh such to worship him. Verse 24 says, “God is a Spirit, and they that worship him must worship him in spirit and in truth.” Truth requires surrender. Spirit requires yielding. Worship requires both. We have learned how to worship with our voices, but God is calling us to worship with our lives.

Worship is not the sound you make; it is the life you lay down. Worship is not the moment you feel; it is the decision to obey. Worship is not the atmosphere you create; it is the altar you climb. The woman with the alabaster jar did not worship because she poured perfume. She worshipped because she surrendered herself.

Her tears were a surrender.
Her breaking was a surrender.
Her silence was a surrender.
Her courage was surrendered.

And Jesus called it beautiful. “She has done a beautiful thing to Me” (Mark 14:6). Not because it was perfect. Not because it was public. Not because it was impressive. But because it was surrendered. This is the fragrance God receives, not the sound of your voice, but the surrender of your will. Worship becomes truth when the heart bows before the hands lift, when obedience rises before emotion stirs, when surrender becomes the offering instead of performance becoming the substitute.

If worship is surrender, what is God asking you to lay down so your worship can become truth instead of performance?

Prayer:

Lord, make my life the worship You desire, not performance, not routine, but a heart fully yielded, fully listening, fully Yours.

CHAPTER EIGHT

WORSHIP AS IDENTITY: BECOMING WHO GOD SEES

Who are you when God calls your name, not who you've been, not who people remember, but who He sees?

Who are you when God calls your name, not who you have been, nor who people remember, but who He perceives you to be? Identity constitutes the foundation of worship. It is not the identity you devised for survival, nor the identity shaped by pressure, nor the identity that pain engraved into your memory. Instead, identity originates in the declaration God spoke over you before your formation. Scripture affirms, "Before I formed you in the womb, I knew you"

(Jeremiah 1:5). Therefore, identity begins with God's awareness of you, His naming of you, and His vision of you before you ever perceived yourself.

However, life possesses a manner of obscuring that intrinsic knowledge. Individuals assign you new labels based on their limitations. Experiences reform your identity in response to their wounds. Failures recalibrate your self-perception in light of their repercussions. Shame redefines you in light of its accusations. Fear diminishes your sense of self according to its falsehoods. Culture recontextualises your identity in line with its expectations. Over time, the original identity bestowed by God becomes concealed beneath the identity imposed by life.

This is why worship is not merely surrender; it is a return. Worship constitutes the journey back to one's original self, prior to worldly influence. It is also a return to the identity God perceived before self-awareness. Furthermore, worship signifies a re-engagement with the voice that bestowed your name before any other had the opportunity. The woman with the alabaster jar entered the room labelled as “the sinner,” yet departed as “the worshipper."

The Scripture states, “A woman came with an alabaster jar...” (Mark 14:3). She was identified neither by her name nor her title, only by her label. But Jesus renamed her without speaking her name. He named her through acceptance. He named her through defense. He named her through honor. “Leave her alone,” He said. “She has done a beautiful thing to Me” (Mark 14:6). Identity is restored in the presence of God.

Abraham became the father of nations not when Isaac was born, but when he obeyed on the mountain. His destiny was confirmed. Moses became a deliverer not when he confronted Pharaoh, but when he turned aside to the burning bush. David became king not when he sat on the throne, but when he worshipped in the field. Mary became favoured not when she carried Jesus, but when she said, “Be it unto me according to Your word” (Luke 1:38). Identity is not revealed in the spotlight. Identity is revealed in surrender. This is why worship is identity:

it aligns you with who God says you are.

When you obey, you step into identity. When you surrender, you step into identity. When you yield, you step into identity. Worship becomes the bridge between who you were and who you are becoming. The fragrance of your life rises from the identity you embrace.

If you perceive yourself as broken, your acts of worship will be marked by timidity. If you regard yourself as unworthy, your worship will be characterized by hesitation. If you believe yourself to be forgotten, your worship will remain silent. However, when one perceives oneself as God perceives, being chosen, called, loved, known, and seen, one's worship becomes courageous. Identity fuels worship, and worship reveals identity; the two are inherently interconnected. This is why the enemy attacks identity first. If he can confuse who you are, he can silence your worship. But God is calling you back to yourself, the self He designed, the self He named, and the self He sees.

What identity is waiting on your obedience, and what part of you is God calling back into alignment with His voice?

Prayer:

Father, reveal who I am in Your eyes. Silence every false identity. Awaken the person You designed before time began. Let me walk boldly in that truth.

CHAPTER NINE

WORSHIP AS CALLING, PURPOSE UNLOCKED THROUGH OBEDIENCE

What if the calling you've been waiting for is waiting on your obedience?

Calling is not something a person pursues; rather, it is something they enter into. The foundational step is invariably obedience. Each significant calling in Scripture commenced with a straightforward instruction, whether a single word, a brief sentence, or a divine prompt, which served as the gateway to destiny.

"Go."

"Follow Me."

"Arise."

"Speak."

"Leave."

"Do not fear."

"Take your son."

"Break the jar."

The instruction served as the gateway, with obedience being the essential key. The calling occupies the room on the opposite side. While we frequently pray for clarity of purpose, it is ultimately God who responds through guidance. We seek a comprehensive understanding, but God provides a singular direction. As scripture states, "Your word is a lamp to my feet and a light to my path" (Psalm 119:105).

A lamp does not illuminate the entire journey; rather, it reveals only the next step.

Therefore, calling is not disclosed in advance; it is revealed through obedience. When he obeyed on the mountain. "Now I know that you fear God" (Genesis 22:12). Moses did not become a deliverer when he confronted Pharaoh; he became a deliverer when he turned aside to the burning bush. "When the Lord saw that he turned aside to look, God called to him" (Exodus 3:4). David did not become king when he wore the crown; he became king when he worshipped in obscurity.

Mary did not become the mother of Jesus when she held Him; she became the mother of Jesus when she said, "Be it unto me according to Your word" (Luke 1:38). The disciples did not become apostles when they preached; they became apostles when they left their nets. “Immediately they left their nets and followed Him” (Matthew 4:20). Paul did not become a world changer when he wrote letters; he became a world changer when he surrendered on the Damascus Road. “Lord, what do You want me to do?” (Acts 9:6).

Calling is not activated by talent. Calling is activated by obedience.

This is why worship is calling: it aligns a life with God’s voice, and God’s voice leads a person into purpose. Your calling is not somewhere far away. It is hidden inside your next yes. Your destiny is not waiting in the future. It is waiting in your obedience today. The fragrance of calling rises when you obey the instruction God has already given you, not the instruction you want, not the instruction you prefer, not the instruction that feels comfortable, but the instruction that confronts you, stretches you, scares you, and requires surrender. Because calling is costly. Calling is disruptive. Calling is uncomfortable. Calling is holy.

Worship is the posture that makes calling possible. When you worship through obedience, you step into the version of yourself God designed.

You step into the assignment that heaven wrote.

You step into the fragrance your life was meant to release. Your calling is not waiting for more information.

It is waiting for more obedience.

What instruction have you delayed that is delaying the calling God has already placed on your life?

Prayer:

Set my obedience on fire. Burn away complacency. Ignite passion, purity, and holy conviction. Let my life blaze with Your purpose.

PART IV

THE RELEASE OF THE FRAGRANCE

CHAPTER TEN

WORSHIP AS LIBERATION: BREAKING INTERNAL LIMITATIONS

What if the greatest prison you will ever escape is the one built inside your own heart?

We often imagine bondage as something external, something imposed by people, circumstances, systems, or seasons. But the deepest limitations are internal. Fear that whispers you are not enough. Shame that reminds you of who you used to be. Doubt that questions every step. Pride that refuses to bow. Insecurity that hides behind competence.

Unbelief that masks itself as caution. Self-protection that builds walls instead of altars.

Old identities that cling to your memory.

Old wounds that shape your reactions.

Old narratives that define your expectations.

These are the invisible chains that keep a person bound even when their life looks free. And here is the truth most people never confront: obedience breaks internal prisons. Not willpower. Not motivation. Not positive thinking. Not self-help. Obedience. Because obedience forces the heart to confront what it has been avoiding. When God gives an instruction, it is rarely about the task. It is about the transformation. The instruction exposes the limitation. The obedience breaks it.

Moses' limitation was fear, and God broke it with a staff and a sentence: "Now go; I will be with your mouth and teach you what to say" (Exodus 4:12). Gideon's limitation was insecurity, and God broke it with a greeting: "The Lord is with you, mighty warrior" (Judges 6:12). Jeremiah's limitation was youth, and God broke it with a touch: "Behold, I have put My words in your mouth" (Jeremiah 1:9). Peter's limitation was instability, and Jesus broke it with a call: "Follow Me" (Matthew 4:19).

The woman with the alabaster jar carried a burden known as shame, which God dispelled through a moment of surrender. "She has done a beautiful thing to Me" (Mark 14:6). Internal prisons are not broken by chance; rather, they are shattered through obedience. Since obedience necessitates courage, trust, vulnerability, surrender, identity, and yielding, and these are precisely the elements that internal prisons oppose.

This is why obedience appears akin to warfare. Not because God is opposing you, but because your limitations are. Fear opposes obedience. Pride opposes obedience. Shame opposes obedience. Comfort opposes obedience. Old identities oppose obedience. However, when you obey despite these obstacles, a supernatural phenomenon occurs: the limitation is broken. The fear diminishes in voice. The shame relinquishes its hold. The insecurity loses its influence. The old identity ceases to have its power. Obedience liberates you from the self that cannot fulfil your calling.

This is why worship signifies liberation: it constitutes obedience, and obedience shatters bonds. Scripture states, "You shall know the truth, and the truth shall make you free" (John 8:32). Truth is not merely information; it is obedience. Freedom is not a sensation; it is surrender. The aroma of your life cannot emanate from a heart that remains confined. It emanates from a heart that has been liberated. Freedom is not emotion.

Freedom is not relief.

Freedom is not escape.

Freedom is obedience.

Freedom is surrender.

Freedom is worship.

What internal limitation is God asking you to break through obedience, and who will you become once it is shattered?

Prayer:

Lord, teach me to value the oil You've entrusted to me. Help me steward it with humility, reverence, and wisdom. Let the crushing produce glory, not bitterness.

CHAPTER ELEVEN

WORSHIP AS COURAGE, STEPPING INTO THE UNKNOWN

Why does obedience require courage, and what happens when God calls you into a place you cannot predict or control?

Obedience is not difficult because the instruction is complicated. Obedience is difficult because the outcome is unknown. The unknown is where fear lives, where doubt whispers, where control dies, where faith is tested, and where courage is born. Every act of obedience requires courage because obedience always leads a person into territory they have never walked before.

Abraham had never climbed that

mountain with such a command resting on his shoulders. Moses had never stood before a king with nothing but a staff and a word from God. Joshua had never marched around a wall waiting for heaven to intervene.

Esther had never approached a throne uninvited, risking her life for her people. Peter had never stepped out of a boat onto water that could not hold him. Mary had never carried a miracle that would change the world. Courage is not the absence of fear; courage is obedience in the presence of fear.

This is why worship is courageous: it is obedience, and obedience requires stepping into the unknown with God. When God calls, He rarely gives details. He gives direction. “Go” (Genesis 12:1). “Follow Me” (Matthew 4:19). “Do not fear” (Isaiah 41:10). “Take courage” (Matthew 14:27). “Launch into the deep” (Luke 5:4). The deep is where courage is tested. The deep is where faith grows. The deep is where worship becomes more than a song; it becomes a life laid down in trust.

Peter did not walk on water because he was brave. He walked on water because he obeyed. Jesus said, “Come” (Matthew 14:29), and Peter stepped into the impossible. Courage followed obedience, not the other way around. This is the mystery: courage is not what you feel before you obey; courage is what rises in you because you obey.

The woman with the alabaster jar was

not fearless when she entered the room. She was obedient. Her courage came after she stepped forward. David was not fearless when he faced Goliath. He was obedient. His courage rose when he moved toward the giant. Scripture says, "David ran quickly toward the battle line" (1 Samuel 17:48). Courage is activated by movement. Fear loses its power when you step. The unknown becomes holy when you obey.

This is why God often calls you into places that stretch you: courage is a fragrance, too. The fragrance of boldness. The fragrance of trust. The fragrance of faith that refuses to bow to fear. Scripture says, "We are the fragrance of Christ" (2 Corinthians 2:15). Your courage becomes worship when you obey God in the face of uncertainty.

And heaven responds to courage. Heaven honors courage. Heaven multiplies courage. Heaven fills the unknown with provision, protection, and presence. You do not need to know the outcome. You only need to know the Voice.

Where is God asking you to step into the unknown, and what fragrance of courage will rise when you obey?

Prayer:

Make worship my posture, my language, my breath. Let every part of my life reflect Your presence. Shape me into a vessel that carries You well.

CHAPTER TWELVE

WORSHIP AS LEGACY: LEAVING A FRAGRANCE IN THE WORLD

What will remain of your life when your voice is silent, your season has shifted, and your journey is complete?

Legacy is not what a person builds. Legacy is what they release. Buildings crumble. Titles fade. Achievements are forgotten. But fragrance remains. The woman with the alabaster jar never preached a sermon, never wrote a book, never led a ministry, never stood on a stage. Yet Jesus stated, "Wherever the gospel is preached in the whole world, what she has done will also be told in memory of her" (Mark 14:9). Her legacy was not her name. Her legacy was her obedience. Her fragrance became her story. Her surrender became her memorial.

This is the mystery of worship: your obedience today becomes someone's revelation tomorrow. Abraham's obedience became a nation. Moses' obedience became deliverance. David's obedience became a kingdom. Mary's obedience became the doorway through which salvation entered the world. Jesus' obedience became redemption for all humanity. Legacy is not what you leave behind. Legacy is what your obedience sets in motion.

Your worship is not just for you. Your surrender is not just for your season. Your obedience is not just for your moment. Your fragrance travels. It moves into rooms you will never enter. It touches people you will never meet. It influences generations you will never see. It becomes a spiritual inheritance. Scripture says, "We are the fragrance of Christ" (2 Corinthians 2:15). Legacy is the aroma of a life yielded to God. And here is the truth most people never realize: legacy is not created at the end of your life. Legacy is created every time you obey.

Every yes becomes a seed.

Every surrender becomes a story.

Every act of obedience becomes a fragrance that rises long after the moment has passed.

Your legacy is not defined solely by your accomplishments. Instead, it is shaped by your alignment, obedience, and worship.

The essence of your life is cultivated through every decision made, every sacrifice offered, every yielding displayed, every step taken into the unknown, and every moment in which you prioritise God above yourself. This is the fragrance that heaven perceives. It is the aroma that the world recalls. Ultimately, it is this fragrance that becomes your enduring legacy. You are not merely living a life; you are emanating a distinctive scent.

What fragrance do you want your life to leave in the world, and what act of obedience is God asking you to release to begin that legacy now?

Prayer:

Father, release the fragrance of my life into the world. Let every yes echo beyond my generation. Use me as You will, for Your glory, for Your kingdom, for Your name.

CONCLUSION

THE FRAGRANCE THAT REMAINS

Some books you simply read, while others read you. This one was never meant to be just read; it was meant to be inhaled. Obedience is not a chapter, surrender is not a lesson, worship is not a concept, and fragrance is not a metaphor. Instead, they are all movements, invitations, and awakenings.

You now stand at the threshold of something sacred; it is not the conclusion of a book but the inception of a becoming. You have traversed silence, rupture, surrender, identity, calling, courage, liberation, and legacy. However, revelation alone does not constitute transformation. True transformation commences with a decision, one that is not necessarily dramatic, public, or perfect, but genuinely surrendered.

Because the fragrance of your life is not released by what you know, it is released by what you obey, and heaven is still leaning toward you. The same Voice that whispered in the silence is still speaking. The same invitation that hovered over Abraham, the woman with the jar, Mary, David, Peter, and every worshipper before you are currently present. It does not require perfection or performance, nor does it demand certainty; it simply requests your affirmation.

A quiet yes. A trembling yes. A courageous yes. A surrendered yes. Because your next yes will release a fragrance you cannot yet imagine, one that will outlive you, touch rooms you will never enter, and become your worship, your legacy, your offering.

This is not the end.

This is the inhale before the next obedience. And so, the final question is not about the book.

It is about you.

What will your next yes release into the world?

AUTHOR'S BLESSING

THE FRAGRANCE THAT FOLLOWS YOU

To all those who have traversed these pages: May the Holy Spirit impart a gentle yet empowering presence upon you. May His presence sustain you as a healing balm and as a force capable of breaking bonds. May every silent aspect within you be awakened once more. May every weary part find renewal and repose.

May all concealed places be revealed in illumination. May every fractured space transform into a portal of splendour. I bestow a blessing upon your ears to perceive God's voice in moments of silence. I pray your heart may say yes, unencumbered by fear.

I invoke blessings upon your hands to pour forth what you have once guarded. I ask for your feet to ascend any mountain that obedience demands.

I bless your spirit to surrender, trust, and ascend. May courage be granted to you. May your identity serve as a resilient anchor. May your calling inspire awakening within you. May freedom surround your existence. May your legacy extend beyond your earthly lifetime.

Furthermore, when the world seeks to redefine you, may God voice of God resound with greater authority. When fear endeavours to silence your voice, may boldness arise like a mighty river. When shame attempts to conceal you, may grace elevate you into the illumination of truth. When limitations seek to restrain you, may obedience set you free.

I commend your affirmation, the silent one, the trembling one, the costly one. May it resonate through eternity. May it forge pathways previously unimagined. May it influence generations yet unborn. May it emanate a fragrance that is recognized and cherished by heaven; earth cannot ignore. May the oil on your life never run dry. May the fire on your altar never go out. May the fragrance of your worship fill every room you enter, and every room you will never see. You are not leaving this book. You are stepping into a new becoming, a new obedience.

A new fragrance.

And may the God who called you, the God who sees you,
the God who walks with you, the God who delights in your surrender, carry you into every yes that is waiting.

May your life smell like worship.
May your journey drip with obedience.
May your legacy rise like fragrance.

And may you never be the same again.

CLOSING PROSE

THE EXHALE OF WORSHIP

You have walked through these pages, through silence and surrender, through breaking and becoming, through identity, calling, courage, and legacy. But this is not where the journey ends. This is where it begins. Every revelation you encountered here was not meant to remain on the page. It was meant to awaken something in you, a fragrance, a yes, a becoming.

May the words you have read echo long after the book is closed. May the prayers linger in the corners of your spirit. May the invitations follow you into your days and nights. May the Holy Spirit breathe on every seed planted in these chapters until obedience becomes your rhythm and worship your life. You are leaving these pages, but not the Presence. You are stepping into a deeper surrender, a truer identity, a bolder courage, a richer fragrance.

May your life ascend before God like fragrant incense. May your affirmations open doors previously unimagined. May your obedience influence generations you shall never see. May your fragrance permeate spaces you shall never enter.

As you proceed, may God walk alongside you, speak within you, and guide you into each subsequent step.

This represents your exhalation.

This signifies your release.

The Fragrance

This marks your transformation.

Proceed in worship.

Proceed in obedience.

Proceed in fragrance.

ACKNOWLEDGMENTS

To the One who breathes revelation, this book is Yours. Every word, every whisper, every insight came from Your presence. Thank You for entrusting me with the fragrance of this message.

To the Holy Spirit, my Teacher, my Guide, my Breath. You carried me through every chapter, every pause, and every moment of surrender. Thank You for the oil.

To my family, thank you for your love, patience, and covering, and for your unwavering belief in the call of God upon my life.

To every spiritual leader, mentor, and voice that has poured into me, your obedience has created pathways for mine. Your fragrance has shaped my own.

To the readers, thank you for opening your hearts to this journey. May your life release a fragrance that transforms generations.

REFLECTION QUESTIONS

1. The Alabaster Box: What are you still protecting that God is asking you to break?

2. The Mountain of Obedience: Where is God calling you to obey without full understanding, and what part of your heart resists surrender, and why?

4. Identity: Which false identities must fall for your true identity to rise?

5. Calling: What instruction have you delayed that is delaying your destiny?

6. Courage: Where is God asking you to step into the unknown?

7. Legacy: What fragrance do you want your life to leave behind?

INVITATION TO CHRIST

If, as you read this book, something has awakened within you, a longing, a stirring, a pull, that is Jesus summoning you home. Worship commences with surrender, and surrender originates from a relationship.

If you desire to know Him, pray from your heart: "Jesus, I surrender. I believe You are the Son of God. I believe You died and rose for me. Forgive my sins. Heal my heart. Make me Yours. Teach me to walk with You, obey You, and release upon me the fragrance You designed for my life. Amen."

If you prayed this, heaven rejoices, and your fragrance has just begun.

SCRIPTURE INDEX

Genesis

Genesis 12:1 — Calling

Genesis 22:1–14 — Abraham's obedience

Exodus

Exodus 3:1–12 — Moses' calling

1 Samuel

1 Samuel 17:48 — David's courage

Psalms

Psalm 119:105 — God's direction

Isaiah

Isaiah 41:10 — Do not fear

Jeremiah

Jeremiah 1:5 — Identity

Jeremiah 1:9 — God's touch

Matthew

Matthew 4:19–20 — The disciples' obedience

Matthew 14:27–29 — Peter walking on water

Mark

Mark 14:3–9 — The alabaster jar

Luke

Luke 1:38 — Mary's surrender

Luke 5:4 — Launch into the deep

Luke 22:42 — Gethsemane

John

John 8:32 — Truth and freedom

John 12:3 — The fragrance filling the house

Acts:

Acts 9:3–6 — Paul’s surrender

Philippians

Philippians 3:8 — Counting all as loss

Philippians 4:18 — A sweet-smelling aroma

2 Corinthians

2 Corinthians 2:15 — The fragrance of Christ

ABOUT THE AUTHOR

Oluwakemi T. Amuda is a distinguished career diplomat, doctoral researcher, strategic communication specialist, and author whose work bridges diplomacy, leadership, and identity. Her life is marked by a deep commitment to serving God and her nation. She is the author of The Diplomatic Leader, The Female Diplomat, and now The Fragrance, a work birthed from deep revelation and a mandate to awaken worship in the hearts of believers.

Kemi's writing is marked by clarity, depth, and spiritual resonance. She serves as a steward of revelation and a voice of alignment. She lives as a vessel poured out, releasing the aroma of Christ to her generation.

NOTE ON ORIGINALITY

This book is not a theological manual. It is a spiritual impartation; a revelation carried in obedience. The insights within these pages were birthed through prayer, Scripture, and the gentle leading of the Holy Spirit. While the biblical narratives referenced are timeless, the interpretations, language, metaphors, and spiritual applications are original expressions given to me through revelation. They are not intended to replace Scripture, but to draw you deeper into it.

May every word lead you back to Almighty God, the author of our life.

www.ingramcontent.com/pod-product-compliance
Lightning Source LLC
LaVergne TN
LVHW010936110826
845149LV00013B/2620